Unlocking the Secrets of Science

Profiling 20th Century Achievers in Science, Medicine, and Technology

Otto Hahn and the Story of Nuclear Fission

Jim Whiting

Mitchell Lane
PUBLISHERS

PO Box 196 • Hockessin, Delaware 19707
www.mitchelllane.com

Unlocking the Secrets of Science

Profiling 20th Century Achievers in Science, Medicine, and Technology

Otto Hahn and the Story of Nuclear Fission

Mitchell Lane
PUBLISHERS

Printing   1   2   3   4   5   6   7   8   9   10

Library of Congress Cataloging-in-Publication Data
Whiting, Jim, 1943-
　　　Otto Hahn and the story of nuclear fission/Jim Whiting.
　　　　　　p. cm. — (Unlocking the secrets of science)
Summary: Profiles German chemist Otto Hahn. whose research into radioactivity led
　　　to the discovery of nuclear fission and, despite his opposition, to the
　　　development of the atomic bomb.
Includes bibliographical references and index.
　　　ISBN 1-58415-204-4 (lib. bdg.)
1. Hahn, Otto, 1879-1968—Juvenile literature. 2. Nuclear fission—Juvenile literature.
　　　3. Chemists—Germany—Biography—Juvenile literature. [1. Hahn, Otto, 1879-
　　　1968. 2. Chemists. 3. Scientists. 4. Nobel Prizes—Biography. 5. Nuclear
　　　fission.] I. Title. II. Series.
QD22.H2W45 2003
539.7'092—dc21   2003008852

ABOUT THE AUTHOR: Jim Whiting has been a journalist, writer, editor, and photographer for more than 20 years. In addition to a lengthy stint as publisher of *Northwest Runner* magazine, Mr. Whiting has contributed articles to the *Seattle Times*, *Conde Nast Traveler*, *Newsday*, and *Saturday Evening Post*. He has edited more than 20 titles in the Mitchell Lane Real-Life Reader Biography series and Unlocking the Secrets of Science. He lives in Washington state with his wife and two teenage sons.

PHOTO CREDITS: cover: Corbis; pp. 6, 10, 12 Corbis; p. 16 Science Researchers; p. 24 Corbis; p. 30 Science Researchers; p. 38 Getty Images.

PUBLISHER'S NOTE: In selecting those persons to be profiled in this series, we first attempted to identify the most notable accomplishments of the 20th century in science, medicine, and technology. When we were done, we noted a serious deficiency in the inclusion of women. For the greater part of the 20th century science, medicine, and technology were male-dominated fields. In many cases, the contributions of women went unrecognized. Women have tried for years to be included in these areas, and in many cases, women worked side by side with men who took credit for their ideas and discoveries. Even as we move forward into the 21st century, we find women still sadly underrepresented. It is not an oversight, therefore, that we profiled mostly male achievers. Information simply does not exist to include a fair selection of women.

Contents

U.S. Army Air Corps pilot Paul Tibbets waves from the window of his B-29 bomber early on the morning of August 6, 1945. He and the crew of his aircraft are about to make history.

Chapter 1

The Dawn of a New Era

It was just past midnight on August 6, 1945, but hardly anyone was sleeping on the Pacific island of Tinian. Ever since it had been captured from the Japanese the previous year, Tinian had been an important Army Air Force base. Almost every day huge B-29 bombers took off on missions to attack the Japanese homeland.

Today another bombing mission was scheduled. Virtually everyone on Tinian knew that it was different from all the others. Instead of the usual dozens of airplanes, it would involve only one. A new, top-secret weapon had been loaded into the bomber the previous afternoon. There was an air of excitement, of anticipation.

The bomber's 12-man crew had already been told that they would be carrying the most destructive weapon that anyone had ever used, though they didn't know the secret behind its awesome power. Now they met for their final briefing. The pilot, Paul Tibbets, reminded them to wear the special goggles they had been issued. The weatherman predicted that the sky over the target would be clear. A chaplain led the men in a brief prayer. Then they had breakfast: ham and eggs and pineapple fritters.

When they were through eating, the men walked out to their airplane. It was brightly lit up. The men posed in front of it. Photographers took their pictures and movie cameramen filmed them.

The crew climbed into the airplane. Tibbets started the engines at 2:27 A.M. He let them warm up for 18 minutes.

Then he called the control tower for clearance. It was quickly granted, because there weren't any other planes waiting.

Tibbets pushed the throttle forward. His airplane, which he had named the *Enola Gay* after his mother, began to roll down the two-mile-long runway. He had made this takeoff many times before. But he was taking no chances. His plane was 15,000 pounds overweight, so he wanted to use almost the entire runway. Part of the additional weight came from extra fuel in the airplane. Part of it came from what was in the *Enola Gay*'s bomb bay.

No one had ever seen a weapon like this bomb before. Nicknamed "Little Boy," it was about ten and a half feet long and two and a half feet in diameter. One of Tibbets' crew members described it as "an elongated trash can with fins." If so, it was the most expensive trash can in the history of the world. It was the final result of the Manhattan Project, the costliest military project the United States had ever undertaken.

Slowly the plane struggled into the air. Soon nothing was below it but the ocean, still black because it was long before sunrise. Tibbets flew at a low altitude for a while. Two weapons specialists were finishing some work in the bomb bay. The air temperature there was a comfortable 72 degrees.

The B-29 was the most formidable aircraft of its day. By the standards of 21st-century jet aircraft, it was slow, traveling at about 300 miles an hour. It took more than three hours just to reach the island of Iwo Jima, which U.S. Marines had captured several months previously. There it met up with two other B-29s. One was an observation plane. The other one would take pictures.

The three planes turned almost directly to the north and began the long flight toward their target. It was the city of Hiroshima, Japan. The men drank coffee and ate ham sandwiches. At 7:30 one of the weapons specialists went back to the bomb bay. He switched on the bomb's electrical circuits.

Tibbets began a long, slow climb to the plane's bombing altitude. At 8:40, six hours after leaving Tinian, they leveled off at 31,000 feet.

Soon the *Enola Gay* arrived over the target. The other two planes fell back. The bombardier looked down at the city six miles below him. He pressed a button to open the bomb bay doors. The city rolled by underneath him. Then he saw a T-shaped bridge. That was the aiming point. He pressed another button. A few seconds after 8:15 local time (an hour earlier than the time that the plane had been keeping), the bomb fell away from the airplane.

Forty-three seconds later there was a tremendous explosion. The plane was more than 11 miles away, yet it was thrown about as if it had been hit by antiaircraft fire. The crew looked back, but they couldn't see the city. An enormous mushroom cloud completely obscured it.

The copilot said, "Where we had seen a clear city two minutes before, we could now no longer see the city. We could see smoke and fires creeping up the sides of the mountains."

Tibbets came on the intercom. "Fellows," he said, "you have just dropped the first atomic bomb in history."

A mushroom-shaped cloud billows thousands of feet into the air moments after the Enola Gay *drops the first atomic bomb on Hiroshima, Japan. The black smoke at the bottom of the picture obscures a scene of unprecedented destruction.*

Chapter 2
An Enjoyable Boyhood

As the *Enola Gay* began the long flight back to Tinian, the airplane left behind death and destruction far beyond anything the world had ever known.

A doctor who survived the bombing recalled that just before the blast, the morning had been "still, warm, and beautiful. Shimmering leaves, reflecting sunlight from a cloudless sky, made a pleasant contrast with shadows in my garden," he recorded according to Richard Rhodes in *The Making of the Atomic Bomb.*

When "Little Boy" detonated soon afterward, there were no shadows in Hiroshima. The flash was so intense that many people were blinded. The heat was so great that many people simply disappeared. No one knows how many people died instantly or in the next few hours, but most estimates are well in excess of 100,000. Thousands more would die in later years of radiation poisoning. Of the city's 76,000 structures, two-thirds were completely destroyed.

The events that culminated in such widespread devastation began late in 1938 in a small chemistry laboratory in Germany. A scientist was conducting experiments with uranium. During World War I, he had been responsible for the deaths of many enemy soldiers. But as he conducted his uranium experiments, he wasn't looking for a way to produce new weapons. He was simply trying to expand human knowledge.

His name was Otto Hahn.

Otto Hahn as he appeared about the time he was awarded the Nobel Prize for chemistry. His discovery of nuclear fission is one of the most important scientific achievements of the 20th century.

Hahn was born on March 8, 1879, in Frankfurt am Main, Germany. His parents were Heinrich and Charlotte Hahn. Heinrich Hahn worked as a glazier, a craftsman who makes windows and the frames into which they are inserted. Otto was the third of the couple's three sons. The eldest, Heinrich, had been born in 1876, and Julius in 1877. In addition, the boys had an older half brother, Karl, from their mother's first marriage, which had ended with the death of her husband.

Otto was born in especially prosperous times. Heinrich Hahn's business soon did so well that he hired several men to do the actual work, while he acted as an overseer and contractor. By the time Otto was one year old, the family was able to move from a cramped three-room apartment into a large house. It had plenty of room for the four boys and for the family business, which was located on the ground floor. The living rooms and kitchen were on the second floor. The boys slept on the third floor, which was not heated. It wasn't unusual for the boys to find solid ice in their washing bowls during the winter months.

Saturday nights were a highlight. It was the boys' weekly bath. The maids would bring up hot water and fill a large zinc tub. Otto and one of his brothers would both jump in with their toy boats and have fierce naval battles. Then they would come down to dinner in their freshly cleaned nightshirts.

When he was six, Otto entered the preparatory department of the Klinger Oberrealschule. At first he didn't do well. As a left-hander, he had a great deal of difficulty with handwriting. But within a couple of years he ranked third among the 40 or 45 pupils. He quickly learned French, and in the meantime handwriting wasn't as important.

One of Otto's primary interests while he was growing up was stamp collecting. He also enjoyed playing card games, backgammon, and chess with his brothers. On Sundays Heinrich and Charlotte would take their boys for walks.

"It was not much fun for us, because there we had to behave like good little boys," Otto recalled in his book *Otto Hahn: My Life.* They much more enjoyed going into the nearby woods with Karl, who allowed his younger siblings to take off their shoes and socks and plunge into the ponds.

With plenty of time to himself, Otto found that he enjoyed reading. Some of his favorite books were adventure stories such as those by James Fenimore Cooper and Jules Verne. He also played the piano and enjoyed going to the opera, where his family had a box.

It wasn't an entirely carefree existence. The boys were expected to help out in the family business, performing such chores as making deliveries to customers and picking up materials that the craftsmen needed.

Otto was a somewhat sickly boy, who at different times suffered from colds, tonsillitis, and serious asthma. Once he came down with diphtheria, which at that time was often fatal. Despite a fever of more than 104 degrees, he slowly recovered. His closest call came when he had pneumonia. For several days he was close to dying, and his recovery took a number of weeks. But after he turned 14, he enjoyed excellent health and was hardly ever ill again.

His father was a nonsmoker and forbade his sons to smoke. The school didn't allow its students to go into taverns. As so often happens, prohibiting these actions only made the boys more eager to try them. As a teenager, Otto spent a lot of time in taverns, where he drank beer and smoked cigarettes and cigars.

Once he was almost caught. He had just returned home from spending an afternoon at his favorite tavern. Because he had recently had a cold, the family doctor was waiting to give him a physical examination. When Otto took a deep breath, the doctor smelled the beer and cigarette smoke, but he didn't say anything.

His two older brothers became apprenticed to their father so that they could eventually take over the family business. Heinrich Hahn enjoyed buying houses and remodeling them, and he hoped that his third son would share the same interest. He wanted Otto to study architecture. But there was a problem.

"I had no talent for drawing, possessed no artistic imagination whatsoever, and altogether was totally unsuited to the profession," he wrote in *Otto Hahn: My Life.*

He soon found an alternative. He had become increasingly interested in chemistry. While he described his teachers as "excruciatingly boring," he enjoyed the subject matter. He began conducting chemical experiments in the washroom at home. His interest increased when he attended a series of lectures given by a man who eventually became a university-level teacher.

He finally asked his father if he could study chemistry. Although Heinrich must have been disappointed, he gave his permission. Despite his newfound passion for chemistry, Otto's three top marks when he took his university entrance exams in 1897 were in gymnastics, singing, and religious instruction. Later that year, Otto entered the University of Marburg, determined to study chemistry.

This photo of Otto Hahn and Lise Meitner in Hahn's basement laboratory at the Chemical Institute at the University of Berlin was taken soon after they met in 1907. At that time, there was still a great deal of prejudice against women working in research. Even though she had a Ph.D. degree in physics, Meitner had to use a different entrance than the Institute's male researchers. Despite many obstacles, Hahn and Meitner worked together for 31 years.

Chapter 3
A Radical Career Change

Otto Hahn didn't know anyone at Marburg. He decided to join a student corps, similar to fraternities at U.S. colleges, in order to make friends.

His first choice was the *Burschenschaft,* or fencing corps. These groups are most famous for the matches they had with each other. The young men wore heavy head guards that exposed little else besides their cheeks. The matches ended when one of the fencers suffered a cut more than an inch and a half long. The one who was wounded could choose whether or not to close the wound in such a way that it would leave a scar. Most chose to display it, and the scars became a sort of badge of honor.

Otto's parents disapproved of the *Burschenschaft,* so their son joined the Natural History-Medical Society instead. On one occasion, however, he did have to fight a duel. As he was passing a fellow student in 1899, the other man called Hahn a "sissy." Under the prevailing student code of honor, Hahn had to challenge him. The weapons were heavy sabers. Though Hahn was left-handed, he was required to hold the weapon in his right hand. In addition, his opponent was much larger. Hahn was fortunate that he only suffered two small scratches on his arm.

The rest of his university experience was more pleasant. He continued his early habits with beer and cigars now that there were no disapproving parents. His corps also had many established rituals about alcoholic consumption, which Hahn didn't have any trouble observing.

"Our attention to science was not very noticeable," he confessed in *Otto Hahn: A Scientific Autobiography.* "Therefore my student days proceeded without worry and with many happy hours. I had no intention of becoming a scientist and assumed that a job in industry required only learning the 'major'—in my case, chemistry."

In 1901, he completed his university education with a Ph.D. in chemistry. Soon afterward he began his year of compulsory military service in the German army. The year concluded with a series of field maneuvers. When they were completed, Hahn believed that his military career was finished, too.

"Probably no one regarded military service as anything but an entirely peaceful duty to the Fatherland and a means of keeping oneself fit," he wrote in *Otto Hahn: My Life.*

As subsequent events proved, he couldn't have been more mistaken. Soon after taking off his uniform, he received a job at the University of Marburg as an assistant to one of his old chemistry professors. Serving in such a position for two years would customarily lead to a strong recommendation for a job with one of Germany's leading chemical companies.

Near the end of this period, Hahn learned that he was likely to be hired by a chemical manufacturer known as Kalle and Company. One of the terms of the employment was that he would occasionally be asked to travel abroad. For this reason, it was necessary to live in another country first in order to become somewhat familiar with the language.

Hahn was interested and left for London in September 1904. He felt confident that when he returned after six months or a year, a job would be waiting for him. The course of his life seemed cast in stone. He would be an industrial chemist, earning a good living.

Once again, he couldn't have been more mistaken.

In London he was assigned to work with the noted chemist Sir William Ramsay, who had discovered several inert gases such as helium, neon, and argon. More recently, Ramsay had turned his attention to radioactivity, the process by which certain elements give off particles and rays. Radioactivity had been discovered in 1896 by a French physicist named Henri Becquerel.

Almost casually, Ramsay asked Hahn to work with radium, a radioactive chemical element that had been discovered six years earlier by French scientists Marie and Pierre Curie. Hahn said that he had no experience with radium. Ramsay replied was that that was just fine. Without any experience, Hahn wouldn't have any preconceived ideas.

Hahn settled into a routine. Soon his experiments turned up what appeared to be a new element. He called it radiothorium because it was closely related to thorium, one of the heaviest known chemical elements.

Several months later Ramsay asked Hahn about his plans. Hahn told him about the tentative job offer back in Germany. Ramsay advised Hahn to stay with radioactivity. As a new field, it was likely to have an outstanding future. Hahn would be getting in on the ground floor.

Ramsay advised him to go to Montreal, Canada, to do further work with Ernest Rutherford, one of the world's leading figures in studying radioactivity. Hahn sent a letter to Rutherford, mentioning the discovery of radiothorium to demonstrate his ability.

Soon afterward, Hahn received a letter from Kalle and Company, confirming the job offer. Though in *Otto Hahn: My Life* he said simply, "I naturally declined, for by now it was clear that radium research was to be my field," turning down the job was an act of courage. He was giving up a steady job with a good income for an unknown future.

His association with Rutherford proved beneficial. While in Canada Hahn discovered yet another new element, which he called radioactinium.

When Hahn returned to Germany in 1906, he obtained a job as a teacher at the Chemical Institute at the University of Berlin. Because radioactivity was still so new, it wasn't as highly regarded as more traditional fields. He was assigned a room in the Institute's basement. It had once been a carpenter's shop. Hahn's position was anything but secure, even though early in 1907 he discovered yet another element, which he called mesothorium.

In *Otto Hahn: My Life,* Hahn explained, "We have become a bit more cautious about the concept 'element.' In fact what is meant is generally just isotopes of the same element, that is, variations with different atomic weights. But at that time both Ramsay and Rutherford used to call them 'new elements.' So, during the initial years of working in the field, I kept on discovering 'new elements.' Rutherford used to say of me in those days: 'Hahn has a flair for discovering new elements.'"

In other words, his discoveries weren't technically elements as we now understand them. However, they marked him as a man whose research methods were innovative and productive.

Later in 1907, Hahn met Lise Meitner, a young woman from Vienna, Austria, who had obtained her Ph.D. in physics the previous year. She came to Berlin to attend lectures by noted physicist Max Planck and originally planned to stay for two years. Those two years would eventually stretch into 31, and her collaboration with Hahn would lead to one of the most important discoveries of the 20th century. But that was far in the future.

When Meitner was growing up, girls were not allowed to attend universities. As a result, her original education had been limited, even though she was obviously a gifted student. Just before the turn of the century, there was a change. Women could be admitted to a university, but to qualify, they had to pass a test called the Matura. Meitner and a few other women took an intensive course of study, trying to cram the equivalent of eight years into two. It worked. Meitner passed the Matura. Because her physics studies at the university included radioactivity, matching her with Hahn was natural when she came to Berlin. The two were close in age and hit it off immediately. The same couldn't be said of Hahn's colleagues.

"At first things were not easy for Lise," Hahn wrote in *Otto Hahn: My Life.* "This was before Emil Fischer [the director of the Chemical Institute] decided to admit women into his laboratory. On the condition that she would never appear in the laboratory, among the students, he gave her permission to work with me in the room that had formerly been the carpenter's workshop."

She could not come upstairs, even to go the bathroom. For that she had to walk to a nearby café.

The following year Rutherford received the Nobel Prize for chemistry for his groundbreaking work in radioactivity. After accepting the award in Sweden, he spent a few days in Berlin. Hahn and Rutherford enjoyed long technical talks. Meitner went Christmas shopping with Mrs. Rutherford.

If she was bitter, Meitner didn't show it. As she recalled in Harry Henderson's *Nuclear Physics,* "When our own work went well we sang together in two-part harmony, mostly songs by Brahms. I was only able to hum, but Hahn had an outstanding voice. We had a very good scientific and personal relationship with our young colleagues at the neighboring Physical Institute. They often came to chat and would sometimes climb in through the window of the 'carpentry shop' instead of taking the usual way. In short, we were young, happy, and carefree."

One reason for her happiness was her close relationship with Hahn. They complemented each other well. He was the expert in chemistry, while the bulk of Meitner's knowledge was in physics.

By modern standards, their association was somewhat unusual. In *Otto Hahn: My Life,* Hahn wrote, "There was no question of any closer relationship between us outside the laboratory. Lise Meitner had had a strict, lady-like upbringing and was very reserved, even shy. I used to lunch with my colleague Franz Fischer almost every day, and go to the café with him on Wednesdays, but for many years I never had a meal with Lise Meitner except on official occasions. Nor did we ever go for a walk together. We met only in the carpenter's shop. There we generally worked until nearly eight in the evening. Lise Meitner went home alone, and so did I. And yet we were really very close friends."

It wasn't all work. Hahn's "outstanding voice" was the result of his joining a local musical group and learning how to sing. He also hiked long trails in the mountains and skied.

In 1911, he had what he would term a "lucky accident."

"The Kaiser Wilhelm Society was founded, and through Emil Fischer I was given the opportunity to form a small department for radioactivity research at the first Kaiser Wilhelm Institute, and Lise Meitner was soon allowed to join my department as a member of the scientific staff," he wrote in his book, *Otto Hahn: A Scientific Autobiography.* "Then things started to expand. The 'Department Hahn' became the 'Department Hahn-Meitner,' then split into 'Department Hahn (Chemistry)' and 'Department Meitner (Physics).'"

Hahn's status finally brought him financial security. The timing was excellent, because 1911 held another significant development for Hahn. In May that year he met Edith Junghans on a steamer cruise. She was an art student in Berlin, and Hahn was immediately interested in her. After the cruise they had very few face-to-face meetings. Nearly all of their courtship consisted of letters. They became engaged a year and a half after their first meeting and were married five months later.

Meanwhile, political storm clouds were building over Europe. In about a year and a half, a terrible tempest would break out.

Fritz Haber was the leader of Germany's research and development of poison gas and other chemical weapons during World War I. Before the war, he developed a method of making chemical fertilizer that still makes it possible for many people to grow enough food to insure their survival.

Chapter 4

Grim Developments

World War I began on August 1, 1914. Germany entered the war with a great deal of confidence. Long trains filled with smiling, laughing soldiers left for the front lines as huge throngs of cheering spectators waved flowers. The atmosphere was highly festive.

Although he was now 35 and a respected scientist, Hahn was quickly recalled to active duty. Like most of his countrymen, Hahn believed not only that Germany was in the right, but also that his country would win—and win quickly.

It didn't. Within a few months, millions of men— Germans on one side, English and French on the other— faced each other in deep trenches, some of them only a few yards apart. Any hope of a quick victory by either side had vanished. Losses were mounting. Sometimes thousands of men would be killed in a single day.

In January 1915, Hahn was ordered to report to Fritz Haber. Haber was a noted chemist who had devised a method for extracting nitrogen from the air to make ammonia. The ammonia would be used to make fertilizer. Because nitrogen is a vital plant nutrient, adding fertilizer that contains nitrogen dramatically improves crop yields. By some estimates, two billion people are dependent on the process Haber invented; without it, there wouldn't be enough food for their survival. Haber would be awarded the 1918 Nobel Prize in chemistry for his discovery.

In 1915, Haber was more concerned with death than with life. He believed that the war's stalemate demanded new weapons. Chief among them would be poison gas.

Hahn protested that using gas would violate the Hague Convention, a series of rules for conducting war.

Haber replied that the French were already using gas in their rifle ammunition. In addition, he argued, using gas would end the war much sooner. Though it would cost some lives, it would save many more. His arguments persuaded Hahn to join him.

After several weeks of training in Berlin, Hahn returned to the front lines. He spent more weeks going up and down the trenches, figuring out the best locations to place the cylinders that contained the poison gas. The weather conditions had to be just right, with a wind blowing from the German lines across to the other side.

Hahn wasn't around on April 22, 1915, when the Germans launched their first poison gas attack. It killed 5,000 men and caused serious injuries to 10,000 more. But it made very little difference to the war. The Germans didn't follow through on the attack, and reserve troops quickly moved up to replace the casualties.

Soon afterward Hahn was transferred to the Eastern Front on the other side of Germany. On June 12 he helped to launch another attack. This time he saw the results of what he had unleashed.

"First we attacked the Russian soldiers with our gases, and then when we saw the poor fellows lying there, dying slowly, we tried to make breathing easier for them by using our own life-saving devices on them," he wrote in *Otto Hahn: My Life.* "It made us realize the utter senselessness of war. First you do your utmost to finish off the stranger over there in the enemy trench, and then when you're face to face with him you can't bear the sight of what you've done and you try to help him. But we couldn't save those poor fellows.

"I felt profoundly ashamed, I was very much upset."

Nevertheless, Hahn continued to work on other gases. Sometimes he risked his life in tests.

"Of course it did take a bit of nerve, but we were specialists, after all, so we were best qualified to estimate the risks," he wrote.

One example of this "bit of nerve" involved the testing of gas masks.

"I was one of the volunteer guinea-pigs who had to wear the mask until the gas penetrated," he recorded in *Otto Hahn: My Life.* "For this purpose we insulated a small wooded hut, which we would fill with an excessively high concentration of phosgene [an especially poisonous gas], and in that atmosphere we stayed until the mask ceased to give protection. On leaving the hut one had instantly to go and take a hot bath in order to remove every trace of phosgene from one's skin and hair."

On one occasion Hahn emerged from this dangerous testing suffering some temporary ill effects. At least one of his colleagues died.

Despite its grimness, the war produced a few lighthearted moments.

As Hahn wrote in *Otto Hahn: My Life*, "During the war I was once introduced to a colonel as a chemical expert and the discoverer of mesothorium.

"'I thought you were a chemist,' the colonel said. 'What business have you to go discovering antediluvian [ancient] animals?'

"Yet mesothorium was only a few years old, and the megatherium about two hundred million years!"

The colonel had confused a chemical element (mesothorium) with a long-extinct ancestor of the giant sloth (megatherium).

Though the war placed great demands on him, Hahn had occasional time off to work with Meitner. These opportunities increased in 1917 when he was transferred to Berlin.

Their work quickly produced results. Early in 1918 they wrote a scientific paper that detailed their discovery of an element they called proto-actinium. With its name shortened slightly to protactinium, it would become the 91st element on the periodic table of elements. First formulated in 1869, the periodic table assigns an atomic number to every element. All atomic numbers are relative to hydrogen, which is number one. The higher the number, the heavier the atom. The highest atomic number at that time, 92, belonged to uranium.

With protactinium, Hahn finally had an element that wouldn't be reclassified as an isotope.

The war ended late in 1918. Hahn took a few months off and then resumed his work with Meitner. Her co-discovery of protactinium and other accomplishments made it impossible for the German scientific establishment to ignore her.

A significant year for both researchers was 1922. Hahn's son Hanno, his only child, was born on April 22. Meitner received "habilitation," a certificate that made it possible for her to finally become a full professor in a German university.

During the following decade, working both independently and together, they became increasingly well known for their accomplishments in radioactivity and nuclear physics.

But once again, political events were about to cast dark shadows over the planet.

Enrico Fermi was an Italian scientist who began conducting experiments in 1934 in which he would bombard the nuclei of atoms with neutrons. A few years later he came to the United States. He quickly became involved in research that led to the development of the atomic bomb.

Chapter 5
Sherlock Holmes in the Laboratory

Adolf Hitler, the leader of the Nazi Party, came to power early in 1933. At that time Hahn was delivering a series of lectures at Cornell University in Ithaca, New York. When the series was completed in the summer, he was invited to take a trip out West.

Meanwhile he had received news about Hitler's harsh new racial laws, so he decided to return to Germany. Some of his associates were being removed from their jobs because of their Jewish backgrounds.

Meitner was one of them. Even though she had converted to Christianity many years earlier, she had been born a Jew. By Hitler's way of thinking, she still qualified as a Jew. She was permitted to continue her research, but she lost her teaching position.

As she explained in Henderson's *Nuclear Physics*, "There was a strong feeling of solidarity among us [Hahn and other scientists]. It was built on mutual trust and this made it possible for the work to continue quite undisturbed even after 1933, although the staff was not entirely united in its political views." Their work would soon take a dramatic turn.

Ever since the discovery of radioactivity and the work of the Curies in the 1890s, scientists had been probing the structure of the atom. Up to that point, atoms had been regarded as the smallest particle in nature. In fact, the word *atom* means "that which cannot be cut any further."

In 1897, British physicist J.J. Thomson discovered the electron. It was much tinier than the atom of which it was a part. Coupled with Becquerel's discovery of radioactivity and the work of the Curies, it showed that the atom wasn't indivisible after all.

The Curies showed that heavy atoms would break down, or decay, over a period of time as they lost particles. Ernest Rutherford and J.J. Thomson wanted to study this process, which was called radioactive decay. They invented a crude "atomic gun," a hollow block of lead that contained decaying radium. It allowed them to study the radioactive particles, called alpha particles, that radium gave off.

In 1911, Rutherford proposed the idea that atoms consist of a dense center called the nucleus with electrons whirling around it in orbits. The nucleus has a positive electrical charge. Electrons have a negative electrical charge. An exact balance between the charges of the electrons and those of the nucleus keeps the atom from flying apart. Rutherford used alpha particles shot from his atomic gun to probe the nuclei of different atoms.

Eight years later, he named the positively charged particles in the nucleus protons. The number of protons in the nucleus determined the atomic number of the element they composed.

Scientists soon realized that this explanation was incomplete. Except for hydrogen, with an atomic weight of one, all the other elements had atomic weights that were twice or even more the weight of their protons. This extra weight couldn't come from the tiny electrons, which were practically weightless.

Rutherford had a theory that there was something else in the nucleus. It would be about the size and weight of a proton, but it would have no electrical charge. Otherwise the nucleus would be unstable.

In 1932, Rutherford's student James Chadwick discovered this particle. He called it the neutron. It had at least one great use: because it had no electrical charge, it was much more useful than alpha particles for probing nuclei. The "bullets" from Rutherford's atomic gun had an electrical charge. Because of this electrical charge, they often were deflected away from the targeted nucleus.

Italian physicist Enrico Fermi quickly seized on Chadwick's discovery. In 1934 he began bombarding the nuclei of the different elements with neutrons, slowly working his way through the periodic table. When he got to uranium, he believed that the nucleus had absorbed the neutrons to create "transuranic elements," elements that were even heavier than uranium. He was wrong.

Hahn, along with Meitner and another chemist named Fritz Strassmann, began experiments similar to Fermi's in 1935. For three years they accomplished little. Then Hahn's long association with Meitner was interrupted.

For several years after Hitler's rise to power, Meitner had been protected from the worst of the attacks against Jews by her Austrian citizenship. Early in 1938 Hitler annexed Austria in what is known as the Anschluss. Suddenly Meitner found herself a German citizen.

She asked permission to leave the country. It was denied. She began to fear for her life. With the help of Hahn and some friends who were living in Holland, she managed to secretly cross the Dutch border and escape from Germany. From Holland, she moved on to Sweden, a neutral country. She was safe.

Hahn and Strassmann continued their experiments. Soon Hahn began observing something strange. As he continued to bombard the uranium nucleus, he noticed that it gave off something that he believed was radium. That was startling. Radium (88) is four places away from uranium (92) in the periodic table. There was no known scientific explanation for such a big change.

Hahn and Strassmann published a scientific paper with their results. Niels Bohr, a prominent Danish nuclear physicist, said that their results were "unnatural." Even worse, Meitner wrote that they were starting to make nonsense. She urged them to check and recheck their results.

Hahn rechecked everything he had done before. Then he added some new techniques. In mid-December, he came upon the truth. The experiments hadn't yielded radium. They had yielded barium.

Barium is chemically very similar to radium, which is why Hahn initially believed that radium had been the result of his experiments. But barium has an atomic number of 56. If uranium turning into radium was "nonsense," how could uranium atoms turn into something just over half their original size? Neither Hahn nor Strassmann could account for that. They sent their results to Meitner.

They also sent a short description of their findings to the German scientific journal *Naturwissenschaften*. Knowing that other scientists were working on the same problem, they wanted to be the first ones to publish their results. The editor immediately cut another article and printed their paper in the January 6, 1939, edition.

In the meantime, Meitner had received Hahn's letter. If it had come from almost anyone else, she probably would have laughed and thrown it away.

As Robert Jungk points out in *Brighter Than a Thousand Suns,* "For over a quarter of a century Lise Meitner and her 'cockerel' (in German, Hahn means cock, or rooster) had worked side by side. Their identities were so closely fused, even in their own minds, that Fraülein Meitner once absent-mindedly replied to a colleague who had spoken to her at a congress: 'I think you've mistaken me for Professor Hahn.'"

This long relationship and close association reassured her that Hahn's methods were thorough and exacting. His findings somehow had to be accounted for.

Her nephew Otto Frisch, a respected scientist himself, had come to visit for the Christmas holidays. He and Meitner went for a walk in the snowy woods and considered Hahn's news. At first Frisch refused to believe Hahn's conclusion. But Meitner's faith in her longtime partner persuaded him to consider it.

"They visualized the uranium nucleus as a waterdrop, barely holding together against the mutual repulsion of its 92 positively charged protons," wrote Richard Rhodes in *Picturing the Bomb: Photographs from the Secret World of the Manhattan Project.* "An incoming neutron would disrupt such an unstable arrangement as violently as if the moon had struck the earth. The uranium nucleus would wobble like a water-filled balloon. On one of its wobbles, elongating like pulled taffy, a neck might form between two bulges. Then the force that held the nuclei together would reassert itself within each bulge, the neck would thin and snap and the two new, smaller nuclei, which might be anything but would usually be barium (atomic number 56) and krypton (atomic number 36) (36 + 56 = 92, the atomic number of uranium), each positively charged, would repel each other with enormous energy—enough energy, Frisch calculated later, to make a visible grain of sand visibly jump."

The famous fictional detective Sherlock Holmes once said, "When you have eliminated the impossible, whatever remains, however improbable, must be the truth."

Every known law of physics dictated that it was "impossible" for a nucleus to undergo such a radical division. But Meitner and Frisch decided that Hahn and Strassmann had just "eliminated the impossible." The "whatever remains," they had to conclude, would shake the scientific community.

The nucleus of an atom could be split.

Frisch conducted further experiments that confirmed Hahn's work. Hahn had referred to the process as the "bursting" of the nucleus. Frisch wanted a different term; he used one from biology. The process by which one cell divides into two is called fission. Frisch gave the name *nuclear fission* to what Hahn had discovered.

No one thought of keeping the news a secret. Several reports quickly appeared in scientific journals. It became obvious that Hahn had stumbled on the tremendous potential energy that Albert Einstein's famous formula, $E = mc^2$, had suggested. (In the equation, E stands for energy, m for mass, and c for the speed of light, which is believed to be a constant.)

Other scientists took Hahn's nuclear fission one step further.

If one neutron would split one uranium atom, that wouldn't release much energy. But the fission would not just create two new atoms. It would also release some extra neutrons. If two of those neutrons could fission two additional uranium atoms, that would release more neutrons. Those neutrons would then fission more uranium atoms. This process would keep on going in a chain reaction. At each step, the number of atoms that were being split would double. After about 80 generations, many millions of atoms would undergo fission simultaneously. It would blow the material apart with tremendous force.

Scientists calculated that one kilogram of uranium (just over two pounds, and about the size of a golf ball) would produce the same explosive power as 20,000 tons of dynamite, a conventional explosive. Most airplanes at that time could carry about two tons of bombs. The same explosive force that would require a huge fleet of 10,000 bombers could be packed into a single airplane.

By then, the swift pace of events had taken nuclear physics far beyond what Hahn and Strassmann had discovered. It was as if they had made a small snowball at the top of a very steep hill and started it rolling down the slope. It would quickly grow larger and larger until it crashed with tremendous force at the bottom of the hill.

Albert Einstein was probably the most famous scientist of the 20th century. When physicists realized the significance of Otto Hahn's splitting of the atom, they asked Einstein to use his prestige to convince U.S. President Franklin Delano Roosevelt of the danger that the United States faced. Einstein was successful, and the country embarked on the Manhattan Project that led to the development of the atomic bomb.

Chapter 6
The Manhattan Project

"Up to 1938, physics had been fun," wrote Alwyn McKay in *The Making of the Atomic Age.* "Now the men in the 'ivory towers' suddenly found themselves custodians of knowledge that could change the course of history." It was early 1939. The world was on the verge of war.

The process Otto Hahn had discovered and Lise Meitner and Otto Frisch had explained could lead to the development of weapons of almost unimaginable destructive capability. The nation that first developed such weapons would have a tremendous advantage. The ones that didn't would be in peril. The nation that developed an atomic bomb first could bury its enemies.

Several scientists who had fled Nazi Germany were all too aware of this fact. They worried that the nonscientists who led the governments of Hitler's enemies wouldn't understand the implications of nuclear fission. They were concerned that Hahn's German background would give Hitler a head start on developing an atomic bomb. In addition, the Germans had taken over Czechoslovakia early in 1939. The country had large deposits of uranium.

They believed that the only hope for the Allies—which included Great Britain and the United States—was to develop an atomic bomb. And they had to develop it faster than the Germans. They approached Albert Einstein—yet another refugee from Hitler's terror—hoping that his enormous prestige would help convince U.S. President Franklin Delano Roosevelt that the danger was very real.

Einstein shared their concern. He agreed to write to Roosevelt.

Roosevelt was sufficiently alarmed. He set in motion a series of events that yielded the Manhattan Project. The project cost billions of dollars and eventually led to the creation of the atomic bomb that was dropped on Hiroshima and another one that fell on Nagasaki three days later. Yet the project was so secret that only a handful of the tens of thousands of people who were involved knew its ultimate purpose.

Until the bomb was successfully tested in a remote desert site in New Mexico in July 1945, the project's leaders were haunted by one fear: they might be too late. As things turned out, they had little reason to be concerned. Hahn intensely disliked Hitler and everything he stood for. He reportedly told a friend that he would kill himself if the result of his years of research was Hitler's having an atomic bomb. He refused to have anything to do with weapons research.

Though other German scientists made some progress, they never came close to developing a bomb. For one thing, building one proved to be much more complicated than originally believed. Another reason is that Hitler, unlike Roosevelt, never seemed to fully understand or appreciate the potential of atomic power. He sometimes even referred to nuclear physics as "Jewish physics"—in his opinion, a belittling comment.

While Hahn stayed away from anything connected with the development of an atomic bomb, he continued to do uranium research during the war years. He couldn't remain out of the reach of the effects of the war, however. The Kaiser Wilhelm Institute of Chemistry, where Hahn worked, was nearly destroyed by a bomb in early 1943. Hahn lost virtually all his important papers. He relocated to another part of Germany and continued his research, though under reduced circumstances.

He was captured by British and American troops at the end of April 1945. He and several German atomic scientists were taken to a country estate in England for questioning to determine the extent of their knowledge about the construction of nuclear weapons. They were still there when Hiroshima was bombed.

According to *The Making of the Atomic Bomb*, U.S. President Harry S. Truman, who became president when Roosevelt died in 1944 and who ordered the bomb to be dropped, said, "This is the greatest thing in history" when he learned of its successful detonation.

Otto Hahn had a considerably different reaction. Neither he nor his colleagues had any idea of the existence of the Manhattan Project or of its success in creating the atomic bomb. "At first I refused to believe that this could be true, but in the end I had to face the fact that it was officially confirmed by the President of the United States," Hahn wrote in *Otto Hahn: My Life*. "I was shocked and depressed beyond measure. The thought of the unspeakable misery of countless innocent women and children was something that I could scarcely bear." His fellow scientists became so concerned that they kept a close watch on him.

Soon after the war, Otto Hahn learned that he had been awarded the 1944 Nobel Prize for chemistry. He was finally able to travel to Stockholm, Sweden, in December 1946 to receive it. It was, and remains, a source of some controversy that Lise Meitner did not share it with him.

Hahn put forth his view of the situation in *Otto Hahn: My Life*. "I really had no responsibility for the course events had taken," he wrote. "The prize had been given to me for work I had done either alone or with my colleague Fritz Strassmann, and for her achievements Lise Meitner had been given a number of honorary degrees in the U.S.A. and had even been declared the 'woman of the year.'"

By then, Hahn had also been appointed president of the Kaiser Wilhelm Society. The victorious Allies soon insisted on changing the Society's name to the Max Planck Society (honoring the famous German scientist) to remove any reference to German militarism. Hahn's towering reputation and complete lack of connections with Hitler made him an ideal leader of the society.

In 1951 Hahn was shot in the back by an inventor who was unhappy with his own lack of recognition. Though Hahn had nothing to do with the inventor's problem, his presidency of the Max Planck Society gave him a high profile. Fortunately, the would-be assassin fired a gun used for stunning cattle, rather than a weapon with real bullets. After a great deal of initial pain, Hahn quickly recovered and resumed his duties.

The following year he was selected for one of Germany's highest honors. He was named to the Order "Pour le Merite" ("for the merit") in Science and Arts. Only 30 German citizens can be members at any given time.

Hahn became a vocal opponent of the use of atomic weapons. He was among the first signers of the Göttingen Declaration in 1957, signifying that he refused to assist in any future German development or construction of atomic weapons. On the other hand, he became a champion for the development of nuclear energy for peaceful purposes.

In 1960 he retired as president of the Max Planck Society. He enjoyed one of the proudest moments of his life when Germany's first nuclear powered merchant ship slid into the water in June 1964. The vessel's name was *Otto Hahn.* In 1966, Hahn, Meitner, and Strassmann were named as joint recipients of the Enrico Fermi Award.

Otto Hahn died on July 28, 1968.

James Chadwick, the man who discovered the neutron, paid tribute to Hahn in the preface to *Otto Hahn: My Life:*

"This exciting discovery of the 'bursting' or 'fission' of uranium owed, to my mind, as much to the character of Hahn as to his great competence as a radiochemist. In all his scientific work one sees his untiring determination to get to the bottom of his problems, his refusal to be satisfied with less than as complete a knowledge as possible of the facts, followed by his acceptance of these facts, however unexpected they might be. Indeed, as he himself has said, more often than not he found something which he had not been looking for. . . . He had an honesty and integrity which commanded the respect and trust of all."

Otto Hahn Chronology

1879 Born on March 8 in Frankfurt am Main, Germany

1897 Begins studies at University of Marburg

1901 Receives Ph.D. in chemistry

1904 Travels to London and works with William Ramsay at University College; discovers radiothorium

1905 Travels to Montreal and works with Ernest Rutherford at Physical Institute of McGill University; discovers radioactinium

1906 Returns to Germany and works with Emil Fischer at Chemical Institute of University of Berlin

1907 Discovers mesothorium; begins collaboration with Lise Meitner

1911 Moves to Kaiser Wilhelm Institute

1913 Marries Edith Junghans

1914 Begins military service in World War I

1918 With Meitner, discovers protactinium

1922 Son Hanno is born

1928 Becomes director of Kaiser Wilhelm Institute for Chemistry

1935 Starts studying the effects of neutrons on uranium with Meitner and Fritz Strassmann

1938 Discovers nuclear fission

1944 Awarded Nobel Prize in chemistry

1945 Captured by Allied soldiers and taken to England

1946 Returns to Germany to begin presidency of Kaiser Wilhelm Institute for Chemistry, then accepts Nobel Prize for chemistry

1948 Is made president of Max Planck Society

1951 Shot in back by unhappy inventor

1952 Becomes member of Order "Pour le Merite" for Science and Arts

1957 Signs Göttingen Declaration opposing German involvement in developing nuclear weapons

1960 Retires as president of Max Planck Society; son Hanno is killed

1964 Launching of the NS *Otto Hahn*, Germany's first nuclear-powered merchant ship

1966 With Fritz Strassmann and Lise Meitner, honored with the Enrico Fermi Award

1968 Dies on July 28

Nuclear Timeline

1803 John Dalton introduces atomic theory.

1866 Alfred Nobel invents dynamite.

1869 Dmitri Mendeleyev publishes periodic table of the elements.

1895 Wilhelm Roentgen discovers X rays.

1896 Henri Becquerel discovers radioactivity.

1897 J.J. Thomson discovers the electron.

1898 Marie and Pierre Curie discover radium.

1900 Max Planck develops quantum theory.

1905 Albert Einstein publishes famous equation $E=mc^2$.

1911 Ernest Rutherford publishes theory of the structure of atoms.

1919 Ernest Rutherford discovers the proton.

1932 James Chadwick discovers the neutron.

1938 Otto Hahn and Fritz Strassmann split uranium atom.

1941 Enrico Fermi proposes hydrogen-bomb theory.

1942 In Chicago, the first chain-reaction nuclear reactor is tested.

1945 First atomic bomb is dropped; World War II ends.

1946 U.S. Atomic Energy Commission is created to manage the development, use, and control of nuclear energy.

1951 First atomic clock, which took two years to build, is fully operational.

1952 Hydrogen bomb is tested for the first time.

1954 USS *Nautilus*, the first nuclear-powered submarine, is launched. The world's first nuclear power plant is opened in Obninsk, Russia.

1957 The world's first commercial nuclear power plant begins producing electricity in Shippingport, Pennsylvania, near Pittsburgh.

1974 Energy Reorganization Act establishes the Energy Research and Development Administration (now part of the U.S. Department of Energy) to oversee military use of nuclear energy and the Nuclear Regulatory Commission to oversee civilian use. These organizations replace the Atomic Energy Commission.

1979 U.S. nuclear power plant at Three Mile Island, Pennsylvania, suffers partial meltdown.

1985 IBM scientists use scanning tunneling microscope to see atoms for the first time.

1986 Accident at Soviet nuclear plant at Chernobyl kills more than 30 people outright and injures thousands.

2000 Nuclear power plants generate 20 percent of total U.S. electricity.

2003 U.S. Navy turns its base on the island of Vieques over to the Department of the Interior, ending 60 years of military testing there. Among the toxic pollutants left behind are depleted uranium shells.

Further Reading

Works Consulted

Fermi, Rachel and Esther Samra. *Picturing the Bomb: Photographs from the Secret World of the Manhattan Project.* New York: Harry N. Abrams, Inc., 1995.

Hahn, Otto. *Otto Hahn: A Scientific Autobiography.* Translated and edited by Willy Ley. New York: Charles Scribner's Sons, 1966.

———. *Otto Hahn: My Life.* Translated by Ernst Kaiser and Eithne Wilkins. London: MacDonald and Company, 1970.

Irving, David. *The German Atomic Bomb.* New York: Simon and Schuster, 1967.

Jungk, Robert. Translated by James Cleugh. *Brighter Than a Thousand Suns: A Personal History of the Atomic Scientists.* New York: Harcourt, 1958.

McKay, Alwyn. *The Making of the Atomic Age.* New York: Oxford University Press, 1984.

McPherson, Malcolm C. *Time Bomb: Fermi, Heisenberg and the Race for the Atomic Bomb.* New York: E.P. Dutton, 1986.

Rhodes, Richard. *The Making of the Atomic Bomb.* New York: Simon & Schuster, Touchstone Books, 1988.

For Young Adults

Bankston, John. *Enrico Fermi and the Nuclear Reactor.* Hockessin, Del.: Mitchell Lane Publishers, 2004.

———. *Lise Meitner and the Atomic Age.* Hockessin, Del.: Mitchell Lane Publishers, 2004.

Beyer, Don E. *The Manhattan Project: America Makes the First Atomic Bomb.* New York: Franklin Watts, 1991.

Biel, Timothy Levi. *Atoms: Building Blocks of Matter.* San Diego: Lucent Books, 1990.

Hamilton, Janet. *Lise Meitner: Pioneer of Nuclear Fission.* Berkeley Heights, N.J.: Enslow Publishers, 2002.

Henderson, Henry. *Nuclear Physics.* New York: Facts on File, Inc., 1998.

Pasachoff, Naomi. *Marie Curie and the Science of Radioactivity.* New York: Oxford University Press, 1996.

Internet Addresses

"The Enrico Fermi Award"
http://www.pnl.gov/fermi/index.html

"The History of Nuclear Energy," Nuclear Engineering, U.S. Department of Energy
http://nova.nuc.umr.edu/nuclear_facts/history/history.html

Manhattan Project Heritage Preservation Association, Inc.
   http://www.childrenofthemanhattanproject.org/index.htm
"Otto Hahn," Spartacus Educational
   www.spartacus.schoolnet.co.uk/GERhahn.htm
"Otto Hahn—Biography," Nobel e-Museum
   www.nobel.se/chemistry/laureates/1944/hahn-bio.html
"Otto Hahn, Lise Meitner and Fritz Strassmann," Chemical Achievers, The Chemical Heritage Foundation
   http://www.chemheritage.org/EducationalServices/chemach/ans/hms.html
U.S. Nuclear Regulatory Commission
   www.nrc.gov

Glossary of Terms

● ●

annex—to include under the domain or a state or country.

atom—the smallest unit that makes up a chemical element.

atomic number—the number of protons in an atom.

atomic weight—the combined weight of protons and neutrons in an atom.

compound—a substance composed of two or more elements, such as water, which is composed of hydrogen and oxygen.

compulsory—required and enforced.

electron—a tiny, almost weightless atomic particle that contains a negative electrical charge and orbits around the nucleus of an atom.

element—a substance that is composed entirely of atoms of one type.

fission—the splitting of the nucleus of an atom.

inert—having no chemical activity.

isotope—a form of an element that contains a different number of neutrons than the usual form.

neutral—not taking sides in a conflict; having no electrical charge.

neutron—a particle, located in nucleus of an atom, that has no electrical charge.

nucleus—the interior core of an atom that is densely packed with protons and neutrons.

periodic table of the elements—the chart showing the position of the elements according to their atomic numbers.

proton—a particle, located in the nucleus of an atom, that carries a positive electrical charge.

radioactivity—the process by which some elements give off particles and rays.

Index